Outsource This Now

How to Triple Your Profits Through Smart Outsourcing

Disclaimer and Terms of Use: The Author and Publisher has strived to be as accurate and complete as possible in the creation of this book, notwithstanding the fact that he does not warrant or represent at any time that the contents within are accurate due to the rapidly changing nature of the Internet. While all attempts have been made to verify information provided in this publication, the Author and Publisher assumes no responsibility for errors, omissions, or contrary interpretation of the subject matter herein. Any perceived slights of specific persons, peoples, or organizations are unintentional. In practical advice books, like anything else in life, there are no guarantees of income made. This book is not intended for use as a source of legal, business, accounting or financial advice. All readers are advised to seek services of competent professionals in legal, business, accounting, and finance field.

Printed in the United States of America

Just to say Thank You for Purchasing this Book I want to give you a gift <u>100% absolutely FREE</u>

A Copy of My Special Report *"Outsource Time"*

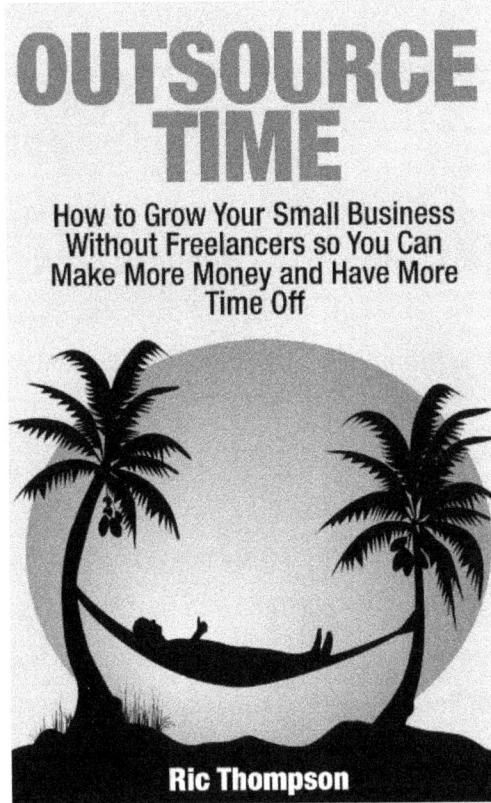

Go to

<u>www.DoneForYouSolutions.com/OutsourceTime</u> **to**

Receive Your FREE Gift

Table of Contents

What You Need to Know First

Congratulations! You're soon going to look back at the decision to download, read, and take action on "How to Triple Your Profits Through Smart Outsourcing!" as one of the best business decisions you've made.

In the coming pages, you're going to learn more about how to outsource efficiently, and leverage the world market of cost effective labor than 99.99% of your fellow business owners – giving you a massive edge in the increasingly competitive and hostile business world.

Before we get into the details of the how-to, in order to unleash the true potential of your business there are some things you need to understand first.

What you need to know will sound very simple, but only the truly successful business owners understand all the finer distinctions of what you're about to read, so pay attention. It's critical to all your success as an entrepreneur.

I hope you're ready!

Here we go...

First:

YOU are NOT your business.

No one person can know everything that's needed for a business to succeed in the world today.

No one person can do everything that's needed for a business to thrive and grow.

No one person has enough TIME to do everything that is needed (even if you knew everything and could do everything)

So let's say that again – YOU are NOT your business. Your business is separate from you and should be larger than what just your efforts can provide.

And to really drive this point home, let's look at the numbers from the US Census Bureau:

The average solopreneur makes $45,687.79

90% of solopreneurs make less than $100,000 per year.

Average of small businesses with under 20 employees? Try ten times the average revenue - $457,205.35

The more people you have working to grow your business, the bigger your business gets – when you do it right.

Now, of course, there are 2 problems with this scenario....

Yes, the cost of labor is the first thing that probably pops into mind. And we're going to spend the whole rest of this report discussing how to cut that down so that you can still grow –hopefully to the point where you can have multiple full time people helping your business grow.

The 2nd problem is the one I want to address here before we go any further...

And it's not a problem that many entrepreneurs recognize at first....

There are very distinct mental and emotional aspects of "YOU are NOT your business" that often don't seem so distinct.

There's often too much overlap between how you view yourself and how you view your business.

Yes, your business will reflect who you are. But a mirror that reflects you is still NOT you.

You only have 24 hours in a day.

Your business can have as many hours as it can afford to pay for.

Time is a very scalable resource for a business. It's NOT for you.

You only *know* so much. Your business needs to "know" far more than you do, in a variety of areas to succeed.

You can only *do* so much. Your business will need to do far, far more than any one individual could ever do if it's going to succeed.

When you don't fully grasp these fundamental truths of business success, you end up getting caught up in the day to day tasks. Your work day starts creeping into your evenings, then weekends start to be sacrificed, your family or friends start getting neglected. You can see where this is headed.

Because it's not just your business – it's YOU who needs to succeed.

And now you're stuck. You identify yourself too closely with your business.

So I invite you to stop heading down that path right now. Step back. Separate yourself from your business.

And if the worst DOES happen, understand this...

If your business fails, YOU are not a failure.

Why?

Because YOU are NOT Your Business.

You can always start another business – as many other successful people have.

> *I've missed more than 9,000 shots in my career. I've lost almost 300 games. 26 times I've been trusted to take the game winning shot and missed. I've failed over and over and over again in my life and that is why I succeed. – Michael Jordan*

Outsource This Now

Ultimately what you need to understand is that in order for you AND your business to succeed at a high level you need to own your business, your business does NOT own you.

That means that you need to know what you should be focusing on and what you should have others do for you.

Look, as the CEO or President of the company there's tons that you absolutely must do that no one else can. But there's a lot left that someone else can and should do.

As a great first place to start, focus on the tasks that are truly high dollar value tasks. New business relationships, creating new streams of revenue, things like that.

Need something more specific to help you?

Then do only those tasks that you can't have performed for less than what your time is worth.

Handling customer email, doing website updates, admin tasks, reports, etc, etc, etc – there's most likely a ton of things that other people can do far more cheaply than you can. They may be even be able to do it faster and better.

The point is again – YOU are NOT your business. You need to separate the two. And now is always better than later.

Exercise

Don't know what your time is worth? You need to. It's going to be critical for your success moving forward. Here's how to figure it out...

Step 1   List your minimum earning target for the year $ _____

Step 2   Divide by # of work hours in the year / _____ =

Step 3   Minimum hourly rate $ _____

Example:

Let's say you work full time in your business (minus 3 weeks a year for vacation), that's 49 weeks.

49 weeks multiplied by 5 days a week equals 245 days.

245 work days a year multiplied by 8 hours a day is 1960 work hours a year.

Make sure you adjust the numbers based on your own work schedule.

So to continue with the example, the calculation for someone working fulltime in their business with a minimum earnings target of $100,000 a year, then divided by 1960 hours a year would be $51.02 an hour.

However, this calculation isn't always a true representation of the value of someone's hour. Most people aren't productive for a full 8 hours of every day. A majority of a person's time is spent on non-revenue producing tasks like checking email, making calls, etc. Yes, these things are needed in every business but they don't necessarily add to your profits. Studies show that average "productive time" is only 10%!

So how do you calculate your value more accurately?

Let's take up the formula again and put your productivity at twice the average number at 20%.

Step 1: List your minimum earnings target for the year
$ _____

Step 2: Multiply your annual working hours with your time productivity percentage ___* __% = _____

Step 3: Divide your minimum earnings by your answer in Step 2 _____ / _____ = _____

Step 4: New minimum hourly rate: $_____

To give an example, your minimum earnings target is $100,000 divided by (1960 working hours a year multiplied by 20%) = $255.10 an hour.

$100,000/ (1960*20%) = $255.10/hour

Your time can actually be worth 5 times more than you think it is!

If you can increase your productivity each day, your hourly value goes up exponentially too!

This calculation shows you how much your time is REALLY worth and so you'd better think twice, even thrice about how you spend that time.

Now, if you're ready to make your business work harder for you and triple your profits, I'll see you in the next section...

Want to really get into why to outsource?

The average full time admin support person or office worker in the US costs $49,320 per year according to the US Bureau of Labor Statistics.

71% of ALL business in the US make less than $100,000 per year in revenue.

NOTE: For any non-business owner person reading this, sales do not equal profits. Sales is the money that comes in before all the different costs from office supplies to keeping your computer running to anything else your business needs to successfully function

So it's simple – the numbers don't add up. Most small businesses simply can't afford NOT to outsource.

And as we've already covered, companies that can leverage the skills, talents, experience and time of other people beyond just the owner succeed at a much higher level.

So NOT having other people involved is not an option for small business owners who want to grow big.

Want to triple the profits you're making now?

You've got to grow your business while increasing your costs as little as possible.

And hiring labor in a pricey labor market like the US would kill the bottom line of your company.

What is outsourcing

Just to make sure we're on the same page, here are some formal definitions of the word outsourcing:

> Merriam-Webster Dictionary: to send away (some of a company's work) to be done by people outside the company
>
> Wikipedia: is the contracting out of a business process to a third-party.

Now, these definitions say nothing about leveraging international labor, just that it's someone outside the company doing some of the company's work.

That means that you can send some of your paperwork to a work-at-home Mom next door to get it all done and you're outsourcing.

You could get a web developer across the country and that would be outsourcing.

So why is it that most people refer to outsourcing as using people in other countries from your own?

Why? The short answer is it's cheaper. Explained in a more formal way, it's because it leverages the principal of Global Labor Arbitrage:

Global labor arbitrage is an economic phenomenon where, as a result of the removal of or disintegration of barriers to international trade, jobs move to nations where labor and the cost of doing business is inexpensive and/or impoverished labor moves to nations with higher paying jobs

By the way, those "barriers to international trade" that disintegrated? Thank the internet for that. Most small businesses aren't looking to offshore their manufacturing plant (they don't have one), they're looking for smart people who are hungry for work with a reliable internet connection who can do it cost effectively.

Offshoring describes the relocation by a company of a business process from one country to another—typically an operational process, such as manufacturing, or supporting processes, such as accounting. Even state governments employ offshoring.

Look, it's simple... since the technology exists to send work to people a very long distance away, why not send it to people who will do it far cheaper than to those who may be closer but charge a lot more for the same work?

We'll discuss potential issues of this in Section 6 Where to Outsource, but for now, let's just make sure we've got the concept covered.

Fortunately, with the internet and technology like Skype, Google Docs and dozens of other cool tools and toys we can work with people around the world. So we're not limited to hiring people from just one labor market. We can pick and choose what labor market to use for our business.

This does NOT mean that outsourcing doesn't have downsides too. But as long as you're willing to learn how to do it right, you'll find that it's a critical piece to achieve the levels of profitability you want.

What Every Small Business Should Outsource (and what NOT to)

Outsourcing is not going to solve all your labor problems. So let's tackle what you can't outsource then get into what you can (and should) outsource.

First, the obvious roles you can't outsource...

1) **Receptionists, wait staff for restaurants, and other people you need to work at your business location dealing with customers face to face.**

2) **Things that absolutely require your presence or unique skill**

3) **The overall direction of your vision. If it's your company – you still have to drive the proverbial bus ☺**

But that leaves a TON of things you can outsource...
- tax reporting
- legal work
- web development and design
- bookkeeping
- customer service
- prospect and client management
- product fulfillment
- data entry
- research
- reports

Tax Reporting

If you have an accountant do your taxes, you're already outsourcing.

If you're doing taxes yourself, you could be making a huge mistake. There are so many tax benefits for businesses that it's almost impossible to know how to utilize them all without being a professional.

Take your last couple of tax returns into an accountant who specializes in small businesses (you definitely want a specialist, not someone who lumps you in with all their other clients – small business is a world of its own). See if they'll review it for you as a way to see if they can earn your business. If they can't save you money, don't work with them. Odds are good a pro will easily make it worth your while in real dollars saved to work with them.

Legal Work

And if you've done any legal paperwork, like create an LLC, odds are good you had an attorney help do some of the work (if not all of it). Again, that's outsourcing – and smart. With everything else we as small business owners need to know how can we possibly know all the legal mumbo jumbo too?

Web Development & Design

People spend entire careers building up skills in this area. How (and why?) would you compete when you can just hire them to do what your business needs?

Bookkeeping

Yes, you've got to know your numbers. But that doesn't mean you have to be the one entering all the data and handling all the basic bookkeeping tasks. Look around, and you'll easily be able to find a freelancer or service to handle this for you. Which is especially great if you're like me and dread doing this type of work yourself.

Customer Service

Let's face it, 80% to 90% of what comes in from emails to phone calls are the same old questions over and over again. Why not create standard answers to the standard questions and let someone else handle this for you? Anything that comes in that truly requires your touch can just be forwarded to you to handle – saving you the vast bulk of the time required for these types of tasks.

Prospect and Client Management

If you've set things up in your business right, there's a system in place to move prospects (and clients!) forward. Even if it's you doing it all right now, odds are really good that there are many steps that could be done by someone else since it's really just a task that's being done over and over again. Get someone pleasant with great communication skills to take this over and free you up to do something even more valuable.

Product Fulfillment

It shocks me when I find someone still handling this themselves. Really? There's so many more valuable things you can do with your time than spend it on simple manual labor. Heck, depending on the product you could even set it up on something like Amazon's Createspace and have them help you market it for more sales.

Data Entry

Is there a more draining task than this one for most people? Yes, keeping your data straight can be critical, but it's not rocket science and it doesn't take the CEO of the company. Even an inexperienced Virtual Assistant can be trained for this.

Research

Yes, this is important. And it's incredibly time consuming. After all, it's not the actual research where your skills and experience are needed – it's the analysis once the information has been gathered. Save yourself the bulk of the time and get some help.

Reports

Repeatable task? You should not be doing it. Get someone else to handle those daily, weekly or monthly reports and then you can just focus your time examining the results. You may be the only one who can make decisions based on the reports, but typically there are a lot of people out there that can put the report together.

And what about Marketing and Business strategies?

No offense intended, but the odds are really good that there are people out there who have more experience and knowledge than you do in building successful businesses. Some of these people set themselves up as coaches or consultants who will help you craft a strong direction for your business to grow.

And now is probably a great time to separate two different levels of outsourcing.

Strategy vs Execution

This is one of the biggest areas of confusion when entrepreneurs first dive into outsourcing.

Some people that you outsource to, like your accountant for instance, handle both levels of work, strategy and execution. They create a tax savings strategy for your business and then they execute them by having their assistant fill out all the proper paperwork.

Makes it easy to have a one-stop shop right?

However, in other areas of your business, you'll need to go to two different sources.

A business consultant doesn't typically also do the work; they just guide you in the right direction. They provide strategy. YOU or someone else you hire does the actual work.

It's critical to understand the difference between Strategy and Execution because you almost never want to go to someone who only handles execution to provide you strategy. And you wouldn't want to pay a person who does strategy to do the execution even if they would because the cost would usually be prohibitive.

For instance, if someone you outsource to is good at building a web page, it does not mean that the same web page will meet your marketing needs. A web developer who can build whatever you need is powerful and required in today's world of business – but that doesn't mean that web developer knows marketing. They're a tech person. You need a marketing person to help you create a marketing strategy for your website. And a tech person to execute the plan.

Strategy is done by experts who understand the big picture of how things are going to impact your business. A worker bee who just executes is there to follow directions that you provide.

Strategy people are experts and you'll be paying for that expertise.

Worker bees are there to execute (get the work done) that the strategy requires- so their time is typically far less expensive.

Be VERY wary of hiring people who do execution to provide strategy. That person from Fiverr or oDesk who claims they can handle your social media for cheap? Are they going to provide you with a social media strategy that works for your business in your industry and compliments your overall business plan? Or are they just going to do some things they know how to do that someone has told them might work?

Strategy is best done by experts who get the "big picture" and how it will affect your unique business.

Once strategy is laid out, there are typically lots of people who can properly execute it.

Hot Tip: From personal experience, many true experts really hate the daily grind of actually doing the work and will charge you far more to do the work than to just create a strategy. Make sure you're not overpaying to have the work done just because you don't want to split strategy and execution. Team up your expert strategist with a cost effective "doer" so it all gets done and focuses each person on your team to their strengths. This alone can triple profits on a project by cutting down massively on expenses.

How to Start Smart

If you've already been outsourcing, I would suggest that you at least skim through this section. There are some proven tips that you might not have heard about and that will save you a ton of time, energy, and money.

And if you're new to outsourcing, take the upcoming tips to heart, starting out on solid footing is a key part in keeping your profits high and costs low.

Over the years I've found out (mostly the hard way) that there are 3 big rules to outsourcing correctly – and most entrepreneurs fall prey to them, sometimes repeatedly.

Ever hear of a small business owner wanting to get a big project done, like say a website, and they find this great solution where everything will get done and it will just be awesome?

So they write a big fat check, then sit back and leave it up to the web company to deliver the goods.

You know what's coming right? If you've been there, I'll cringe with you.

The check gets cashed and six months later there's still no site. Or there Is a site but it's nothing like what was promised.

And of course it's NOT just websites – that's just a common one.

You see, it's because small business owners don't know Rule #1 to outsourcing smart...

Rule #1 - Start Small

And ironically, not starting small is the source of the biggest amounts of lost time, energy and money.

That website solution that didn't turn out and you had to hire someone else to come in and pick up the pieces (or worse – you just dropped it)? If that whole debacle had been avoided by starting small, the project costs would have been a fraction of what they ended up at, the timeline would have been greatly reduced, and your profits far, far higher.

Look, when working with a new outsource solution – whether an individual or a team, you must, must, must follow Rule #1 Start Small.

Test the new provider you've found with a small project, or at least give yourself an "out" after a small milestone has been set.

Sticking with the website project – sure, you'd like that outsourcer to handle the whole project. It would make your life easier if you didn't have to find another solution right? But you need to find out FAST if they ARE going to work out.

So have them start on something small. Maybe just design the site's homepage as the first step. And give them a reasonable amount of time to get it done.

The whole rest of the project is contingent on how they do on that first small step.

After all, if they can't do that small part right, who wants them to handle the whole project?

The benefits to this are HUGE. Not only are you risking a small fraction of your overall budget because you're only going to pay for that small part, not the whole project, you're also going to find out far faster if that solution provider meets your standards and time requirements or not.

After all, what's faster? Waiting for the solution provider to try to build an entire website or just design a home page?

Lost time IS lost money. So if you can find out in a week or two instead of months that it's not going to work out, you just regained a TON of time that can be used more profitably.

Of course the solution provider is going to want you to commit to the whole project, that's how they make their money – but you need to protect your interests. Make sure that with any new provider you have a way to start small and over the years what you save in terms of lost time and money are going to be an immense boost to your bottom line.

Now as a cautionary word of advice when applying Rule #1, let's get into…

Rule #2 Pay attention to the HOW, not just the WHAT

Ask yourself this…

If you've never worked with someone before, and neither one of you has the ability to read minds, what are the odds that the results are delivered exactly as you want them the first time around?

Slim to none.

Look, you can argue all you want about how if the person is an expert they should be able to produce the results (The "WHAT") that you want right away. But the challenge is always one of communication. Are you able to clearly communicate to them exactly what you want done the first time around? Is the way they are used to communicating in alignment with yours?

Maybe, maybe not.

So what happens most of the time is that the initial results reflect the communication between the small business owner and the outsourcer, not the skill of the outsourcers themselves.

And then what happens is that the small business owner, not seeing the exact results they want, gets frustrated thinking the outsourcer is an idiot, and moves on to test someone else (or worse, things no one put he can do the project right and stops looking for help altogether). In essence they, "throw the baby out with the bathwater".

Instead of focusing 100% on the "WHAT" you want to have happen, pay attention to the "HOW".

You see, if the provider is the right fit, they can be trained to give you the results you desire. Give them some feedback, add some details to your instructions and they can be cranking out exactly what you want in no time.

But skillset is just a fraction of what makes someone a good fit for you.

HOW they do the work is even MORE important to judge in the beginning than results.

How do they communicate with you? Are they asking intelligent questions? Are they easily available to talk with you?

How is their attitude? Are they pleasant? Respectful?

How hungry are they for your work?

How is their timeliness? Are they meeting deadlines? Are they waiting until the last second and then making excuses?

> **"How you do anything is how you do everything."**

Through years of experience I've found this to be true. At the beginning of a relationship, if a person doesn't complete a project on time because of a "family emergency" you can bet your last dollar that they have a LOT of family emergencies, and your work will always be the last priority.

Walk away.

If you give instructions and you never hear from the person until just before the deadline, you don't get what you expected, and they say, "Well I didn't understand XYZ part of your instructions, so I just winged it." You can bet, once again, that attention to detail and communication are not their strong suit.

Walk away.

Here's the ugly truth: No matter how "good" a person's skills, if they aren't able to properly communicate with you, or if they aren't nice to work with, or if they're blowing deadlines, or if they simply just don't seem to care, you will never be able to "fix" them.

Walk away.

On the other hand, someone who meets all your "HOW" criteria, even if they are not as good skill-set wise, will be far more profitable to you in the long term. You can train them to get the results you want (or give them the tools to train themselves) – but you will never be able to change them into someone you want to work with – they have to come that way.

Which brings us to Rule #3...

Yes, it can be a pain to have to go through a lot of potential outsource providers to find one that really works. But don't fall into the trap of thinking this one person will now be your personal business savior and solve all your problems.

In short...

Rule #3 - Spread the risk around – don't focus on ONE person.

I get it. I really do. It would be SO much easier if one person could handle all the things you don't want to, or don't know how to, or what you just don't have time for.

A right hand person, an executive assistant, a silver bullet to solve all your problems.

It's all too tempting. But like anything else that sounds too good to be true, this is too.

Because there are only 2 ways this is going to turn out.

The first scenario goes like this.

Like you, they are only one person. They only have so much time in the day, so many skills, so much experience. In the end, they just can't, or won't, do all the things you need them to do. They either leave or (worse, stay, and you don't realize how much is NOT getting done) and all too often your business is left in a worse state than when you started.

The second scenario goes like this.

The relationship DOES work out... for a while.
And what you've just done is create a ticking time bomb...

Because life always has a way of intervening. Health problems, family problems, better job offers, or whatever else, are at some point GOING to happen.

So, the one person who's been handling basically your entire business is now gone. And with it, everything comes to a crushing halt. Nothing can get done and you're back at the beginning having to start all over.

The answer is to always focus on building a team. Yes, life will interfere with them too, but if most of your business can move forward while you're replacing a single member of the team, you're far, far better off.

After all, what's going to negatively impact the bottom line more? Overcoming some delays and problems replacing a single member of your team or having to replace the one person who pretty much was your entire team?

That's why rule #3 is "Spread the risk around – don't focus on ONE person."

Where To Start

So now that you know the 3 big rules, where exactly should you start with outsourcing?

If you can start the right way, you'll be able to greatly reduce the risk of lost time, energy and money so pay close attention.

The short answer is to outsource whatever will give you the biggest leverage right now. The biggest "bang for your buck" so to speak.

Still need help?

Whether you've outsourced before and are wondering what to get done next or are brand new to the process, the best advice I can give is to decide for yourself the answer to this question:

What would you rather have right now Time or Money?

It's a hypothetical question, and I'm not saying you can't have both.

But if you HAD to choose just one, right now, what would it be.

Time?

If you answered Time because you're going crazy with everything you have to do then here's what you need to do:

Find out where your time is going right now on a daily and weekly basis and use that as a guide for what to outsource next.

If you can free up your time, imagine the impact that could have on the more important things you could do like get more clients, build more business relationships, or maybe even simply improve the quality of your life and that of your family.

So where does your time go now?

What are you doing that someone else could be doing instead?

What are you doing that the CEO / President of a company really shouldn't be doing?

And after you have a list of things, ask yourself this question:

What is the single biggest thing I could have someone else do that would impact my time the most?

Money?

If your preference is to impact the bottom line and make more money then go through a similar process, but with revenue in mind.

What would be the biggest things that if done, would bring more revenue to the company?

You could have a list that has all sorts of things from building or redoing a web site, to having a weekly newsletter for your clients, to getting a new product ready for sale.

Then ask yourself this:

What one project has the most potential to positively impact the bottom line the fastest?

No, there aren't any guarantees in life, but play the odds. What is most likely to succeed?

That's where you start: Wherever has the most potential to make the biggest impact the fastest.

NOTE to small business owners new to outsourcing: If you've never outsourced, there IS a learning curve in how to delegate. It's not typically knowledge you're born with and I don't know of any schools teaching it so here's a tip:

It might be best if you start outsourcing something YOU are already doing. You don't have to, but if you outsource something you know how to do, it's far easier and faster to explain or train someone else than if you start outsourcing something you don't know how to do.

In other words, there IS a learning curve to outsourcing. So if you add that curve to another curve – like what you have to do to have a good website, you've just added an incredible burden to your first outsourcing project. If you outsource what you know, you can much more quickly see results because you can much more quickly beat the outsourcing learning curve.

The 6 Biggest Mistakes to Avoid

Mistake #1 – Outsourcing the wrong things

Over and over again I see small business owners start outsourcing with the mindset of wanting to get things done from their "To Do" lists. They figure that they can't get them done, so maybe if they outsource them, they can get rid of that overriding guilt for not doing it themselves.

The problem is, they've not taken the time to step back, look at their To Do list and actually ask whether or not those items are truly important in the overall big picture.

Let's face it, you're bringing on costs when you start paying someone else for their time and skills to help build your company – no matter how cost effective it is.

So is that task you want to outsource going to bring in a return? Is it truly important to get that done now versus later?

Is it really the best use of the time you're paying for?

Take that extra moment to look at the big picture and see if this is the most important thing you should be focusing on right now.

You're about to add costs that impact the bottom line. You want the efforts of what's being done to also impact the bottom line,

otherwise tripling your current profits is going to be a lot harder
☺

Mistake #2 Thinking that Your Time = Importance

It's a classic mistake of what holds small business owners back.

Small business owner goes to work, knocks out a 10 hour day and thinks they must have had a productive day.

The problem is that the owner is not an employee. It's not a matter of putting in the hours or punching the clock. It's whether or not their time was being used strategically.

In short, it's the difference between those 10 hours being used on important things, or just being used.

And all too often, the small business owner is getting things done, they're just not truly important things to the overall long term growth of the company.

Look, yes, there are a lot of things that need to be done in a business. The question lies in whether or not YOU have to do them.

There are tons and tons of things that only you can do as the leader of the company. It's your vision, it's your drive that will move everything forward. Who else is going to think up solutions to pressing problems? Who else is going to create new growth strategies for your company?

So just because you are putting time into your business, it doesn't mean that what you are doing is actually important.

Remember, you only have 24 hours in a day. Your business can have as much time as it needs.

Mistake #3 (and probably biggest): Not focusing on your strengths.

You started your business because you have a gift to offer. Something of value that you can provide to others.

If you are spending your time on mundane daily tasks instead of what you are really good at – what's the point?

Sure, daily emails, customer requests, order fulfillment, etc, etc, etc all have to be done. They are important to the successful running of your business – but that does not mean that it's important for YOU to do.

Remember, you are the CEO of your business - the visionary that is in charge of where things go. You are the ONLY one who can do certain things in your business. That could range from building new business relationships to creating new products, to any number of other high impact activities.

If your time is spent on the mundane tasks, the high powered activities aren't getting done.

If your time is spent on the mundane tasks, your true gifts aren't being tapped into.

If your time is spent on the mundane tasks, you aren't leveraging what you were planning on bringing to the table in the first place when you started your business. And if that's not happening, why would anyone choose you over your competitor? What unique value are you bringing to the table for them to have them choose your business over another?

So focus on your strengths and remember that while an activity may be important for your business to get done, it doesn't mean YOU have to do it. You have only 24 hours in a day, your business can have as many hours as it needs.

Mistake #4 Not knowing your numbers

Business is all about numbers. I'm going to assume you watch the big ones like revenue versus expenses so we won't cover that here. But there's another number that most small businesses don't even think to watch...

Your staff costs.

Sure you know how much your staff costs are (probably). But what percentage of your revenue figures are your staff costs?

Typically, a healthy business doesn't spend more than 30% of revenue on staffing costs.

Now, that's not necessarily true for start-ups since sales figures aren't mature and having staff is basically part of your start up investment.

And yes, different industries are different and you will want to hit the internet to research the numbers for your industry, but in general, 30% is a good rule of thumb.

So take your monthly revenue figures, grab your monthly staffing costs and do the math. What percentage are you spending on staff? And does it need to be trimmed?

If your staff costs can be reduced to a manageable amount you've not only made your business future far more secure, you've raised your bottom line profits.

Mistake #5 Communication with outsourcers

If you've ever outsourced before, or had staff, or even raised kids, what I'm about to say makes sense. If you haven't done any of that – pay close attention, what I'm about to say will save you HUGE amounts of time, energy and yes – money.

When working with someone new for the first time, what do you think the odds of some sort of miscommunication happening?

Super high right? Like it would be almost impossible for it NOT to happen.

So remember this when you're pissed off that the new outsourcer didn't do exactly what you wanted them to do the very first time you worked with them.

Odds are really, really good that you had something to do with that lack of perfection.

Usually it's because you weren't clear enough.

I see it all the time. The small business owner makes some sort of assumptions about what the new outsourcer knows about their business, their industry their way of doing things, how the small business owner thinks or communicates, or any number of other assumptions that in hindsight explain why a breakdown occurred.

No matter how talented, experienced and expert a person is – if they've never worked with you before, communicate with them as if they are a 6th grader.

This is NOT to demean them, but if you pretend you're talking to a 6th grader about your business, odds are much better that you are going to communicate all the details and explain things as simply and as clearly as you can.

Now I'm not saying you have to do that permanently. I'm saying you do that at first.

Over time, the communication process will smooth out (usually very quickly) and you'll come to meet them at a middle ground.

Long term (assuming you get through the short term), you'll find that you start forming a more seamless communication process and things will get much better. It can become what you were looking for in the beginning – to work with someone who "gets it".

Just remember that in the beginning, if they've never worked with you before, they aren't going to "get" you, your business, how you communicate, how you think, or pretty much anything else except what they are already good at.

SIDENOTE: If the staffer is virtual don't rely on just emails to communicate. While a written record of communications can be very handy, sometimes nothing beats a live conversation.

Skype is a free tool that can't be beat for these situations. Skype to Skype calls cost nothing even if the staffer is halfway around the world from you. If you want, video calls can even be done so you can see their body language as they talk but beware – video takes a lot more bandwidth and will be less reliable than voice calls.

Mistake #6 Not preparing for transitions

Let's get this out in front, right now...

This awesome person that you kissed a lot of frogs to find, that you invested untold amounts of time to get them up to speed on your business and how you like to do things, at some point is going to be gone.

They. Are. Not. Permanent.

So instead of being shocked, hurt or betrayed, and having your business come to a screeching halt while you find a replacement and then bring them up to speed, how about you take a few steps to be prepared in advance to ease all of that.

Now this is in no way saying you're trying to send a message to your staffer you expect them to leave. You're not trying to "attract" that outcome simply because you choose to be prepared. It's simply good business.

Here's what to do:

1) Document all activities each staff member does for you

   If you don't know what each staff member does, when one leaves it can be difficult to replace them.

2) Document HOW each task is done

We use the term Standard Operating Procedure (SOP).

Most operations in your business are a process. It's repeatable. So document them. When doing X, what's step 1? Step 2? What resources are needed? What's it going to look like when it's done?

This can take the form of a Word doc, a video walk through, an audio recording, whatever makes sense – but you need to have these for everything possible.

Look, let's walk through an example.

Scenario A

Staffer leaves your company. It's a little unclear everything they did although you have a pretty good idea. Nothing however is documented. Again, you have a pretty good idea so hey, how important could it be?

When new staffer comes on, YOU now have to train them. You also run the risk that weeks or months later some small tasks that used to be done are no longer getting done because the old staffer who left used to handle them and the new person was never trained.

Ramp up time? Huge. Not just for them, but because YOU have to train them on every single thing they need to know.

Maybe you have someone else do the training. That's better, but you're still paying DOUBLE –for the new person and whoever is training them.

Scenario B

Staffer leaves your company. There's a complete list of tasks and position description explaining at a high level what the person did. Everywhere possible there is a completely documented SOP for each of the tasks they performed.

New staffer comes on and you get to point them towards the list of tasks, the accompanying SOPs and say "GO!"

Sure, you need to stay on top of them. Maybe review the tasks, check to make sure the first few times they are doing it right. But now we're taking a fraction of the time you (or another staffer) has to spend on the transition.

Transition time is also usually shorter here. And the faster they get up to speed, the less costs you have during transition time.

The fewer costs in transition time, the more that gets added to your bottom line.

3) Have access to everything

Do your staffers have email accounts? Logins to any business services your company uses? Passwords to company accounts?

Track this on an ongoing basis.

Not only will you need to be able to possibly pass these off to the next staffer who replaces them, you may very well want to change them ASAP after the staffer leaves.

Even if you think the staffer left on good terms, it makes sense to reset all passwords to all systems just to be safe.

And if they had an email account where they handled any kind of correspondence for your company, you'll want to make sure you (or your new staffer) has access to that so nothing gets lost in transition.

If some client or potential client is lost because their communication is lost, that's going to make it harder to triple your profits.

Where to Outsource

There are a few different ways to answer the question "where to outsource". Remember that the definitions of outsourcing are:

Merriam-Webster Dictionary: to send away (some of a company's work) to be done by people outside the company

Wikipedia: is the contracting out of a business process to a third-party.

What this means is that you don't have to find overseas labor to outsource. You can just send the work to a neighbor next door who's a contractor. No reason at all to deal with someone half way around the world, in a different culture, who may not speak English as well as you.

However, assuming you're outsourcing to someone who's not close to you geographically, the technology is the same to keep in communication with that person.

Skype for voice or video calls. Google Drive to store documents in the cloud that you can both access and edit. Email for obvious reasons. And if you need to, an FTP program to upload large files to your server so others can access. There are plenty of other tools as well, but those are the basic "must haves".

So if the technological tools don't differ, and there are some major financial advantages to outsourcing to different countries why not?

Virtual Assistants (VAs) in the US typically start at $25 to $30 an hour (this is often for a newbie VA). Average VAs can be $50 an hour, and ones with specialized skills can be up to $100 an hour. Those are fine for special projects here and there, but imagine spending $50 an hour for an ongoing administrative helper. Most small businesses can't come close to affording that.

So for a fraction of that cost, you can go overseas. Whether you hire direct (which will take longer, be more effort, but will typically also be cheaper), or use a service, overseas labor is almost guaranteed to be super cost effective in comparison.

If tripling your profits is the goal, you've got to go overseas for the bulk of your outsourcing then.

But where? What areas of the world are best?

The most popular areas are India and the Philippines. China gets mentioned briefly as they do so much offshore manufacturing, but the language barrier is going to typically be much, much higher. Eastern Europe can also be solid, but tends to be hit or miss. Sometimes you have to weed through a lot of people to find one that can communicate at a high level.

Remember, historically both India and the Philippines have a large influence from English speaking countries – England in India and the US in the Philippines. As a matter of fact, the Philippines has two national languages – one of them being English (perhaps it's more accurate to say American English)

So let's focus on those two areas moving forward.

The next challenge is culture.

Each country has its own distinct cultural influences. And you'll have to be aware of them to successfully interact with an outsourcer from that area long term. India's culture is a proud ancient one that resisted a lot of the English influence put on it during the colonial period. The Philippines has a unique blend of many different cultures that have come in over time including Asian, Spanish and lastly American. Those combined with the core Philippine culture you find a people that thrive in adapting – so well so that there are more Filipinos outside the country than in.

My personal experience in outsourcing to the Philippines has been overall very positive. Not everyone speaks English at a high level, but many do. As a plus, the American influence helps to create a bridge between the two cultures – and make no mistake, the American culture is definitely different from everywhere else in the world. That's not a good thing, and it's not a bad thing, but it IS something you must be aware of and take into consideration.

Finally, the people in the Philippines are very pleasant to deal with. Almost to a fault. They're going to go out of their way to solve problems and take care of things so that they don't have to bring you any bad news. The flip side of that is that they so dislike bringing you bad news, they may not – thereby making things worse. Like with any outsourcing solution, clear communication channels will solve that but it's something to be aware of.

Finally, the economic differences....

What we found out is that India, being the favorite outsourcing place first, quickly caught on to the fact that a lot of US dollars were to be had. So prices quickly rose to where it was cheaper than having work done in the US, but not by as much as you'd expect. They definitely seem to be aggressive in getting as much as they can for what they do. If you're watching the numbers, it can still be a great place to outsource, but definitely pay attention. Typically a lot of tech type outsourcing goes there.

In the Philippines, you see a bit of a different economic situation. A lot of jobs are provided by call centers as major companies use the language skills and pleasant demeanor of the Filipino culture to their advantage. Company names you'd recognize like Dell, Bank of America, HSBC, etc. They work night shift in a cubicle frequently with hours of commute time a day – and consider it a good job. Working for you, possibly from home (saving hours a day in commute time, the gas, etc) is a great job, and if they can make a bit more than at a call center (which is not hard for even tiny US businesses to pay) then it's a great win-win situation.

As you can probably guess, I'm a huge fan of outsourcing to the Philippines for all the reasons above and more. I'm certainly not saying other geographic areas don't work – because they do and I have outsourced to just about all of them – but all things considered, to me, it's far easier to get it to work in the Philippines.

Lastly, no matter where you outsource you always to have to be careful of the person you select to work with you. Just like human beings all over the world, we are all unique. Some of us get along with others better. Some of us are more mature than others. Some of us have better work ethics and attitudes than other. As long as you keep that in mind when getting your outsourcer, you'll go a long ways to having success.

Now how do you actually go about finding someone? Or a team of someones?

First, get clear on what you really need by asking yourself some questions...

Do you need an "internal" team or an "external" team?

What does your company really need to have done?

Is it an occasional project on a single type of task like graphic design?

Maybe you just need a part time graphic designer you can farm out the work to as an "external" outsourcer. Maybe you need a couple of different people to do different types of tasks on an as-needed basis. If so, you really just need a list of outsourcers you can go to when you need them.

Is it someone to help handle admin tasks like emails, customer service, etc for a part or full time basis?

Then you need someone "internal" that knows they are working for you on an ongoing basis every week. Do you have a lot of this kind of work now or coming up fast? Then you need a full internal team.

(We'll cover more about this type of solution in the next Section, but don't skip ahead there's still a lot of ground to cover in this one.)

After you've decided what you need, that will impact where you go to find those people.

For instance...

1. **Fiverr** – for simple projects that you only occasionally need. Great place to go for one-off type projects that are cost effective. Even though everything is $5 US, you can find options for multiples of $5 so definitely worth a search.

2. **Odesk / Elance / Freelancer** - Great for larger projects, or part timers. Typically people looking for full time gigs are not on these sites, but anything can happen.

3. **Staffing / VA services** – for full time staff. Most companies focus on one VA at a time and so if you need multiple people still be prepared to kiss a lot of frogs in the process, not just to find people that will work well for you, but that can work well with each other.

4. **Job boards, Directories, Craigslist, etc.** – These types of resources are for if you're going to hire direct. You'll be doing all the interviewing and testing to make sure the staffer is a good fit, and you'll be dealing with all of the administrative aspects of hiring. This will typically be cheaper than using a service, but you'll be paying up front in terms of time and energy to find the right person as you have to do everything yourself.

5. **Virtual Team Company** – where you can access an entire team of people that are used to working with one another, all at one go. Saving you time, money and effort in getting a flexible team for your small business. (We'll cover this option more in the next Section)

And while you're going over all this, remember that you need to be looking ahead to achieve success in the future too...

If you're interested in tripling your profits, you have to be thinking about tomorrow and not just today. You need to set up a system, an infrastructure that will pay off long term.

For instance, all too often, small business owners are way too focused on the project they have to get done right now. Understandable of course, but let's face it, you're going to have a never ending stream of projects for the rest of your business career. Doesn't it make sense to handle the process of building up a team with that in mind?

Even if you only occasionally need that outsourcer – keep in mind that it's probably going to be for more than just this one project. Don't fool yourself by thinking short term. So when you test someone out for this project you've got right now, don't just rely on whether or not they are ok for this one project – are they someone you want to work with them on a long term basis?

Your Next Step...

Now let's put this all together into a very simple action plan to get you started off the right way so you're on track to triple your profits through outsourcing...

Your 5 Minute Outsourcing Action Plan

Companies should spend no more than 30% of revenue on staffing (and preferably only 20% if possible)

What is your monthly revenue?_____

(If your monthly revenue is erratic, use your annual revenue divided by 12)

20% of that is _____   30% of that is _____

Now that your monthly budget is set, let's get into what you need to have done.

What are the tasks / roles you need to have filled that you can't do yourself? And is it a project or an ongoing thing?

* _____ Ongoing / Project based

* _____ Ongoing / Project based

* _____ Ongoing / Project based

What are the tasks / roles that you need to have filled because you shouldn't be doing them? (What tasks are you doing that as the owner of the company you shouldn't be doing?) And is it a project or an ongoing thing?

* _____ Ongoing / Project based

* _____ Ongoing / Project based

* _____ Ongoing / Project based

What are the tasks / roles that you need to have filled because you don't like doing them? And is it a project or an ongoing thing?

* _____ Ongoing / Project based

* _____ Ongoing / Project based

* _____ Ongoing / Project based

Now, if your budget is too low for all of this right now, we need to prioritize.

What item from the lists above would be the SINGLE biggest possible return for your company if it was done?

It may be hard to pick one, and of course, no one has a crystal ball but what is really holding your company back? Or what project would most likely boost the bottom line of your company the fastest?

While everything can eventually be handled, if you can focus on boosting your bottom line, that increases the budget to outsource next month so you can expand more and get more done, but your eye has to be on the bottom line first.

Once you have the information above sorted, we need to determine the best place to get you some outsourced help.

Choose what description fits you best from the list below:

A)	You have a lot of ongoing work – whether a role that requires full time staff or a lot of ongoing projects where you need access to a number of part-time staff to handle.

B)	You have ongoing work needs (multiple projects, ongoing admin or customer service work, etc) but not enough to hire full timers.

Do you need someone local or does it matter?

If local, check out Craigslist.com or other local directories (even the job wanted ads). Just be clear that this is not an employee position – it's a "contractor" or "outsourcer" position.

If you don't need someone local, your budget will go a lot father typically and you can start looking at more places. If you have a lot of time and want to deal with the hassle, hiring direct can save you money. Just remember there's definitely going to be a much larger investment in time, energy and effort. If you don't want to deal with that, and can pay just a bit more go with a service. You'll be up to speed much faster.

C) The work you need done is mostly just a few small one time projects.

If this is you, my suggestion would be to focus on sources like Fiverr.com, Elance.com or Odesk.com. Again, pick the project that would most likely make the biggest impact to your bottom line, give a small piece to several outsourcers and test.

If you are an A or a B...

There is a special solution out there that may be right for you. A staffing "short cut" if you will.

It won't be for everyone, but if you have a need for ongoing work, and this fits into your monthly budget of at least $300, it's something that could be a great tool in your toolbox for tripling your profits through outsourcing.

It's called **Virtual Team Hours**.

The concept is this...

You "rent" a team that already exists to get your work done.

The people have already been selected and hired, they already work together so you know chemistry isn't an issue and they're not project based workers who are spending more time looking for other projects than working on yours.

Basically, all the hard part has been done for you, AND you only use them as much as you need – thereby limiting your expenses and keeping your profits higher.

Sound good?

Here's how it works...

You select the number of hours you need to get done in a month. That could be as low as 20 hours, or it could be hundreds of hours. It doesn't matter if the roles are full time or part time or a mix.

If the amount of work you need done changes every month, that's fine too as long as you do have ongoing work.

You are then provided access to an entire team of people ranging from web developers and designers to admin staff to customer service to other virtual assistants and beyond.

If you need web development this month, admin work the next month and customer service the next month, that's fine – it all comes down to the hours of work you need. If you need a customer service team every month – that's perfect too.

My company Done For You Solutions is the only team in the world to offer this powerful and flexible approach to staffing. I've already done the hard work of putting together the teams, and I take care of replacing people as need be. All that's left is for you to put that team to use in your business.

To find out more, or to get started today, go to http://www.doneforyousolutions.com/getstarted/ or email us at Support@DoneForYouSolutions.com

How did it go?

We'd love to hear from you with your outsourcing stories, ahas, and reviews! Writing a customer review on Amazon today (http://www.amazon.com/dp/B00H4HHY56) will help spread the word and encourage others to simplify their lives, make more money, and have more time off. Thanks!